香港國際詩歌之夜 *2015*
INTERNATIONAL POETRY NIGHTS IN HONG KONG

編輯 Editors

北島 Bei Dao

陳嘉恩 Shelby K. Y. Chan

方梓勳 Gilbert C. F. Fong

柯夏智 Lucas Klein

馬德松 Christopher Mattison

宋子江 Chris Song

目錄 Contents

Un ciel rouge animal   **6**
紅色動物天空
A red-animal sky

La douleur a ses secrets   **12**
憂傷也有秘密
Grief has secrets

Je pouvais aller vite   **18**
我本來可以走得更快
I could have moved faster

Car le ciel était vrai   **24**
因為天空曾經真實
Because the sky was real

Faire le ménage de ça   **27**
打掃房間去吧
Need for house cleaning

Rentré dans ma tanière   **30**
回到我的隱居洞穴
Walking back into my den

1–12   **33**

衣田·拉朗德
Étienne Lalonde

Un ciel rouge animal

Dimanche se balance
Calmement sous ta peau

On dirait un arbre mort
Le jour pendu aux branches

Un ciel rouge animal
Cherche la fin de chaque chose

Quelqu'un se dit
Le chef de l'automne
Pour mettre fin au vent

Il touche ton front
Le feuillage meurt

Un oiseau crie dur et brillant

Dans la pièce, un mur blanc
Des voix tachées de cendre
Le réveil de nos rêves

Et le cri solitaire de l'oiseau
Pris dans la peinture noire

紅色動物天空

星期天晃晃蕩蕩
靜悄悄在你皮膚下面

就像一棵枯木
日子在枝葉間擺盪

紅色動物天空
尋找每件事情的結局

有人說自己
是秋天的主人
好讓風停止

他觸碰你的前額
葉子漸枯

一隻鳥兒啼聲清越嘹亮

房間裏一堵白牆
聲音沾滿了灰
我們的夢將醒

鳥兒的孤鳴
陷在黑色顏料裏

（黃峪　譯）

A red-animal sky

Sunday on scales
Is calm under your skin

Like a dead tree
The day hangs from its branches

The red-animal sky
searches for the end of everything

Someone claims to be
The leader of Autumn
To put an end to wind

His fingers on your forehead
Leaves dying

A bird caws clear and harsh

In the room a wall white
Of voices tarnished by embers
The awakening of our dreams

The solitary cry of a bird
Stuck in black paint

(Translated by Hugh Hazelton and Antonio D'Alfonso)

La douleur a ses secrets

En cela, même à genoux
Être beau comme un train

La douleur mange de tout
Elle a bien des secrets

Une odeur d'herbe coupée
Détruit tout ce matin

Les montagnes se désistent
Ou demeurent immobiles
Sur le point de tomber

Le silence doit alors
Émettre un signal
Entouré de chaleur

Écoute septembre dehors

Les arbres nus

Prennent des poses

Auxquelles le brouillard consent

憂傷也有秘密

在那裏面，甚至在膝蓋裏
英俊得如同一列火車

憂傷甚麼都吃
她也有不少秘密

剪草的氣味
今早殺死了一切

群山退後
或者變得靜止
即將跌倒

那麼寂靜必須
更改它的訊號
被熱力圍繞

在外傾聽九月

樹木赤裸著

擺 出 姿 勢
為 了 霧 的 首 肯

(黃峪　譯)

Grief has secrets

In that, even on bended knees
Being handsome like a train

Grief eats anything
It has many secrets

The scent of cut grass
Kills everything this morning

Mountains stand back
Or become motionless
About to tip over

Silence must then
Transmit its signal
Cushioned by heat

Listen to September outside

Trees naked

pose for
the consenting fog

(Translated by Hugh Hazelton and Antonio D'Alfonso)

Je pouvais aller vite

J'ai tremblé
Éclosion

J'ai éteint la lumière
Qui faisait non des yeux
Secouant chaque automne
Dans la chambre à démons

À heure fixe
J'ai attendu l'accident
Avec mon sommeil léger
Mon bruit pas tellement mieux
Plein de trous

Je pouvais aller vite
Lumière

Même quand je me réveillais
Sur les murs
Je me laissais couler
Avant de m'envelopper dans l'air

Dans la nuit

Du noir frais au rire fauve

Avec des éclairs

我本來可以走得更快

我顫抖
漸漸綻放

我熄了燈
它剛才正用眼睛說不
每個秋天都搖晃
在魔鬼的房間裏

正在這個時候
我聽到這場意外
而我正在淺睡
我的噪音也不見得更好
它佈滿穿孔

我本來可以走得更快
光亮

即使開始甦醒
在牆壁上
我也會讓自己滾滾
然後陷入空氣的懷抱

在夜裏
黑暗假笑得清涼
閃電划過

(黃峪　譯)

I could have moved faster

I quivered
Blossoming

I shot the light off
Which was nodding no with its eyes
Shaking every autumn
In the devil room

At the right moment
I heard the accident
In my restless slumber
My noise no better
Riddled with holes

I could have moved faster
Flare

Even awakening
On walls
I would let myself roll down
And into an envelop of air

During the night
Darkness is cool with its musky smile
And lightning

(Translated by Hugh Hazelton and Antonio D'Alfonso)

Car le ciel était vrai

Puis, j'ai eu une étoile
Un nom, une collision

Car le ciel était vrai

Il n'était pas de moi

Échec, rideau, rappel

Les dimanches ont le dos large

Allez, imaginez
La nuit masquée maintenant

Une rue, un arbre, un trou

Noir cruel, étouffé

J'ai l'air fou, arraché

C'est peut-être pour mon bien

Un rire creux comme avant

因為天空曾經真實

那時我曾擁有一顆星星
一個名字，一次撞擊

因為天空曾經真實

它非我所有

失敗，窗簾，回憶

星期天慷慨大方

來吧，繼續想像
夜晚現在蒙上面具

一條路，一棵樹，一個洞

殘酷的黑，窒息了

我貌似瘋狂，被綁架

這可能對我更好

笑聲空洞一如過往

(*黃峪　譯*)

Because the sky was real

Then I was given a star
A name, a collision

For the sky was real

Did not belong to me

Failure, curtain, recall

Sundays are generous

Now, go on, imagine
The night with a mask

Street, tree, hole

Darkness cruel, smothered

I look mad, kidnapped

Maybe it's for my own good

Laughter as hollow as passing

(Translated by Hugh Hazelton and Antonio D'Alfonso)

Faire le ménage de ça

Les cris, l'après-midi
Faire le ménage de ça

L'air peut aller plus vite
Du revers de la main

Une plante en tant que voisin

L'heure a le droit de dire non

Au secours

Un cadre, un portrait

Qui peut hanter plus loin

Dérouter nos fantômes

打掃房間去吧

尖叫　下午
打掃房間去吧

空氣會流通得更快
把手翻轉之後

一棵植物當作鄰居

時間有權利説不

救救我

一副相框　一張肖像

能夠繼續縈繞

讓我們的鬼魂走上歧路

(黃峪　譯)

Need for house cleaning

The screaming, the afternoon
Need for house cleaning

Air moves faster
With back of hand

House plant as neighbor

The hour has the right to say no

Help me

A frame, a portrait

That could haunt the beyond

Leading our ghosts astray

(Translated by Hugh Hazelton and Antonio D'Alfonso)

Rentré dans ma tanière

Me nier, me trier
Rentrer dans ma tanière

Mon esprit était calme
Ensoleillé presque
Avec le ciel à la recherche
D'un sourire neuf, brillant

Nuit du printemps qui dort

Cette splendeur agitée
Mal fanée
En moi

Déboîter le regard
Chemin

Comme la lumière
Démon

回到我的隱居洞穴

自我否定　自我分類
回到我的隱居洞穴

我的心情安寧
彷彿充滿陽光
與天空一同尋找
鮮活燦爛的笑容

春天睡去的夜

這光輝騷動不安
衰敗褪色
在我裏面

道路
讓目光失向

惡魔
就像光明

(黃峪　譯)

Walking back into my den

Denying myself, sorting myself out
Walking back into my den

My spirit was calm
Sun-filled like
With sky in search of
Crisp smile, bright

Spring sleeping night

Splendor fidgeting
Improperly fading
In me

Dislocating sight
Road

Like the light
Demon

(Translated by Hugh Hazelton and Antonio D'Alfonso)

1.

La femme prit un bâton
Brassa le feu, murmurant
J'offrirai à mes rêves d'autres destinations

Elle y resta longtemps
Tout devait disparaître avec la première neige

Les désirs
Les mensonges
Les soupirs des fantômes

Déserte, elle abandonna la braise
Comme on se défait d'un amour encombrant
Désireuse de laisser le silence en désordre

Elle avait tout perdu, sauf l'hiver

1.

婦人拿起棍子
捅著爐火，喃喃自語
我將為我的夢想改變方向

她在那裏待了很久
一切都將在初雪落下前消失

那些慾望
那些謊言
那些鬼魂的竊語

被人遺棄，她留下爐中餘燼
就像擺脫糾纏不清的愛人
想把寂靜留在無序當中

她失去了一切，除了冬天

（黃峪　譯）

1.

The woman took a stick
Stirred the fire, murmuring
I'll offer my dreams other destinations

She stayed there a long time
Everything would disappear with the first snowfall

The desires
The lies
The ghosts' whispers

Deserted, she abandoned the embers
As you'd slough off an unwanted love
Wanting to leave silence in disorder

She'd lost everything, except the winter

(Translated by Hugh Hazelton and Antonio D'Alfonso)

2.

La plupart de ses mots traînaient une atmosphère
Le froid comme une épée

De la terre gelée, ils menaçaient le soleil
Pour que le brouillard se taise

Jeté du nord, l'air paraissait plus mince
Atlantique

Un épais voile de neige

La lumière du matin restait bonne à tout faire

2.

她的話語多半在空氣中流連
寒冷像一把劍

在凍結的土地上，他們脅迫著太陽
為了讓霧安靜下來

從北方怒號而來，風似乎變得稀薄
大西洋畔

雪卷成的厚帘

晨光為一切做好準備

(黃峪　譯)

2.

Most of her words trailed along an atmosphere
The cold like a sword

From the frozen earth, they threatened the sun
So the mist would be silenced

Hurled from the north, the air seemed thinner
Atlantic

A thick veil of snow

The morning light remained ready for anything

(Translated by Hugh Hazelton and Antonio D'Alfonso)

3.

Les soupirs encore chaud
Il refusait d'attendre
Il forma un poing pour sentir son souffle
Et s'assurer des mots qui partaient du réveil

N'approche pas de la lumière

La voix partait de lui

Les murmures en lieu sûr
J'ai mes traces dans la neige
Pour me faire une raison

3.

他的嘆息還是暖的
他拒絕等待
握著拳頭試著感受他的呼吸
然後確保這些詞語來自清醒

別太靠近燈光

聲音自他而來

在安全地帶的呢喃
我在雪地裏留下了蹤跡
為了讓自己泰然處之

(黃峪　譯)

3.

His sighs still warm
He refused to wait
Made a fist to feel his breath
And make sure of the words that came from awakening

Don't go too near the light

The voice came from him

The murmurs in a safe place
I've got my tracks in the snow
So I'll have to accept it

(Translated by Hugh Hazelton and Antonio D'Alfonso)

4.

Toi
Le bleu
Toi
La mer
L'amoureuse invisible
Des malades de la mort
Fleurs jeunes
De toi sur moi
Ombres
Nuages
Portés
La pleine lune rebondit
Née pour vents
Et pour cordes
La nuit respire ta peau

4.

你
藍色
你
海洋
看不見的愛人
在為死亡而瘋狂的人們當中
年輕的花朵
來自我上面的你
影子
雲彩
帶來
滿月的重圓
為風而生
為弦而生
夜呼吸著你的皮膚

(黃峪　譯)

4.

You
The blue
You
The sea
The invisible lover
Of those mad with death
Young flowers
Of you on me
Shadows
Clouds
Carried
The full moon rebounds
Born for winds
And cords
The night breathes your skin

(Translated by Hugh Hazelton and Antonio D'Alfonso)

5.

Elle tremble
Nue
Dans l'obscurité

Elle dit
J'irai mieux demain

Se rendre pâle au printemps
Sans quitter les traces
De ses cris dans la neige

La langue au nord de tout

Elle joue la tendresse
De se vouloir humaine

5.

她顫抖
赤裸
於黑暗之中

她說
我明天會更好些

春光下她變得蒼白
並未留下任何痕跡
關於她在雪中的哭號

在一切以北的語言

她裝作溫柔體貼
似乎渴望成為人類

(黃峪　譯)

5.

She trembles
Naked
In the darkness

She says
I'll be better tomorrow

She's pale by spring
Without leaving the tracks
Of her cries in the snow

Language to the north of everything

She plays at the tenderness
Of wanting to be human

(Translated by Hugh Hazelton and Antonio D'Alfonso)

6.

Les regards laissent des trous
Des traces

Lumière froide
Fatiguée

Nuit mangée
Peu de bruit
De colère
Effacée à coups de poings

Soudain une chaise tombe
Et arrive comme un choc

Un son sec
Jour de pluie

La peur pendue aux yeux
Nous nous tournons vers l'air

Affirmer

Être une porte

Un oubli

Un désert

6.

那些眼光留下穿孔
留下痕跡

冷冷的光
疲倦了

被吃掉的夜
很少聲音
來自憤怒
被拳頭敲打而抹去

一張椅子突然倒下
如同休克來臨

乾燥的聲音
雨水的日子

恐懼掛在眼裏
我們轉身向著空氣

確定
是一扇門
一場遺忘
一片沙漠

(黃峪　譯)

6.

The looks leave holes
Tracks

Cold light
Tired

Night eaten
Little noise
Of anger
Obliterated by punches

Suddenly a chair falls
And lands like a shock

A dry sound
Day of rain

Fear hanging in our eyes
We turn toward the air

To claim
To be a door
An oversight
A desert

(Translated by Hugh Hazelton and Antonio D'Alfonso)

7.

Il n'y avait pas de vent
Et le toit de la maison était
Une pièce manquante du ciel

Les fleurs de la literie
Tombées sèches au plancher

Le compte complet du vent

Le soleil manquait d'air

Il neigeait des mouchoirs
Et elle voulait rentrer

Une couverture de laine
Plonger dans un miroir
Retrouver le sommeil

7.

並沒有風
而房子上的瓦
是天空缺掉的那片

臥具上的花朵
枯落在地板上

風的整個故事

太陽也需要透透氣

手帕如雪從天而降
她想要回家

一張羊毛的被子
穿入鏡子裏
睡意重新降臨

(黃峪 譯)

7.

There wasn't any wind
And the roof of the house was
A missing piece of sky

The flowers of the bedding
Fallen dry on the floor

The wind's complete account

The sun needed some air

It was snowing handkerchiefs
And she wanted to go back

A woolen cover
Plunging into a mirror
Able to sleep again

(Translated by Hugh Hazelton and Antonio D'Alfonso)

8.

Des visages
Des vies pleines

Des désirs enneigés

Sinon l'île de corail
Du grésil dans l'entrée

Je suis l'hiver monté
Le soir dans une armure

Les doigts fées
Les doigts chats

Au nord, le noir déparle

Tu as encore pris froid

8.

眾多臉孔
那些充實的生活

那些被雪覆蓋的慾望

要麼就是珊瑚島嶼
在入口的小冰雹

我是冬天的佈景
穿著盔甲的夜

仙女的手指
貓的爪子

在北方，黑暗話語冗長

你又著了涼

（黃峪　譯）

8.

Faces
Full lives

Snow-covered desires

Or else the coral island
Hail in the entryway

I'm the winter set up
In an evening suit of armour

Fairy fingers
Cat fingers

In the north, the darkness rattles on

You've caught cold again

(Translated by Hugh Hazelton and Antonio D'Alfonso)

9.

Sur le chemin gelé
Le soleil poignardé

Je ne serai pas longue
Je vais tout nettoyer

Le temps se couvre

J'ai fait le lit pour ce soir

Est-ce la route
Est-ce l'hiver dans ma voix qui dépasse

Je commence quelque part
J'ai mes draps, mes fantômes

9.

在結冰的路上
太陽被刺傷

我不會待太久
我會全部擦乾淨

天空陰雲密佈

我已經為今夜鋪好了床

是這條路麼
是我漸遠聲音中的冬天麼

我從某處開始
我帶上了我的床單，我的魂魄

(黃峪　譯)

9.

On the frozen road
The stabbed sun

I won't be long
I'll clean up everything

It's clouding over

I've made my bed for the night

Is it the road
Is it the winter in my voice that goes beyond

I'm beginning somewhere
I've got my sheets, my ghosts

(Translated by Hugh Hazelton and Antonio D'Alfonso)

10.

Passer l'hiver, dit-il

Litanie
Chant coupé

Rivières
Douleurs brisées

Là où les glaces se mordent
Le silence a pris froid

J'ai compris

Je ne crois pas

Pont des soupirs
Deuil
Frimas

Jusqu'ici
Peur de tout

10.

度過冬天，他說

連禱
誦唱截斷

河流
破碎的痛

在那裏冰噬咬自己
寂靜著涼傷風

我是懂得的

我並不相信

嘆息的橋
悲悼
白霜

至此為止
害怕一切

(黃峪　譯)

64

10.

Spending the winter, he said

Litany
Chant cut off

Rivers
Broken pains

There where the ice bites itself
The silence caught a chill

I understood

I don't believe

Bridge of sighs
Mourning
Hoar frost

Up to here
Fear of everything

(Translated by Hugh Hazelton and Antonio D'Alfonso)

11.

Le fleuve tarde
La lune perce
Fait son nid
En dents de scie
Sur le chemin usé
Le printemps dépasse
Ne sait pas dessiner
Le bonheur frais lavé
Arraché de ton lit
Se fabrique un sourire

11.

河流遲遲
月亮穿透
造它的巢
在鋸齒裏
在被踏遍的路上
春天突顯而出
不知道怎麼畫出
這種幸福，它剛被洗淨
從你的床上拉下來
唯有塑造一個笑容

(黃峪　譯)

11.

The river takes its time
The moon pierces
Makes its nest
In saw teeth
On a worn path
The spring sticks out
Doesn't know how to draw
Happiness freshly washed
Torn from your bed
Invents a smile

(Translated by Hugh Hazelton and Antonio D'Alfonso)

12.

Le sommeil se retourne

Des marteaux
Sur le toit

Une lune sale
En hiver

C'était sinon sa joie
Courant en sens contraire

Le désir
Au bas mot
De la bonne épaisseur

12.

睡意迴轉

錘子
在屋頂上

骯髒的月亮
在冬天裏

如果不是因為這歡愉
奔自相反的方向

那慾望
至少
有著恰好的稠度

(黃峪　譯)

12.

Sleep returns

Hammers
On the roof

A dirty moon
In winter

It was even its delight
Running the opposite way

The desire
At the least
For the right thickness

(Translated by Hugh Hazelton and Antonio D'Alfonso)

衣田・拉朗德，加拿大魁北克詩人。1999 年以年僅廿歲之齡出版詩集《我是食人族》以及《仍是戰爭》，後者進入「艾塔・特雷絲・聖—蘇比絲詩歌獎」的決選名單，並在「雅克琳・德利—莫崇詩歌獎」評審中獲特別嘉許。2010 年出版的詩集《大自然的故事》獲得2011 年「菲利斯—勒可樂詩歌獎」。另著有詩集《漸老》(2011)、《暗巷》(2012)、《維維爾・克勞德》(2013) 等，後者獲得「埃米爾・內里根詩歌獎」以及「蒙特利爾詩歌節獎」。從2000 到2012 年，拉朗德一共獲得五次魁北克文藝協會獎金和一次加拿大藝術協會獎金。拉朗德曾任紐約的魁北克工作室駐留作家，亦參與過俄羅斯、印度及丹麥等地舉辦的國際詩歌節。

Étienne Lalonde, originally from Montreal, Quebec (Canada), released his first two poetry collections, *Je cannibale* and *C'est encore la guerre*, in 1999, at the age of twenty. *C'est encore la guerre* was a finalist for the Estuaire Terrasses Saint-Sulpice Prize for Poetry and also received a special mention for the Jacqueline Dery-Mochon Prize for Poetry. *Histoires naturelles*, published in 2010, was awarded the 2011 Felix-Leclerc Prize for Poetry. His critically acclaimed book *Devenir vieux* came out in 2011. In 2012, Lalonde published *Chemins mal éclairés* and, in 2013, *Vivier, Claude*, finalist for both the Émile-Nelligan and the Montreal Poetry Festival Prizes for Poetry. From 2000 to 2012, Lalonde received five grants from the Conseil des arts et des lettres du Quebec, as well as one from the Canada Council for the Arts. He was a writer-in-residence at the Quebec Studio in New York and has taken part in international poetry festivals in Russia, India and Denmark.

出版 Publisher
香港中文大學出版社 The Chinese University Press

封面影像 Cover Image
北島 Bei Dao

出版日期 Date of Publication
二零一五年十一月 November 2015

國際書號 ISBN
978- 962- 996- 739- 0

香港國際詩歌之夜 2015 International Poetry Nights in Hong Kong 2015
主辦單位 Organizer
香港中文大學文學院 Faculty of Arts, The Chinese University of Hong Kong

協辦單位 Co-organizers
香港中文大學中國文化研究所
Institute of Chinese Studies, The Chinese University of Hong Kong
香港中文大學出版社 The Chinese University Press
香港兆基創意書院 HKICC Lee Shau Kee School of Creativity
廣州時刻文化傳播有限公司 Moment Communications

贊助 Sponsors
香港法國文化協會 Alliance Française de Hong Kong
上海廿一文化發展有限公司 Shanghai 21 Culture Promotion Co., Ltd.
中國會 The China Club
香港文學出版社有限公司 The Hong Kong Literary Press Co. Limited
斑馬谷文化發展（北京）有限公司 Zebra Valley Culture Development

Printed in Hong Kong